WEEKLY MEDITATIONS

WEEKLY MEDITATIONS

Paul Sédir

FRIENDS IN SPIRIT

First published in French as
Méditations pour Chaque Semaine
A.-L. Legrand, Éditeur
Sotteville-lez-Rouen, 1925
First English edition © Friends in Spirit, 2024
an imprint of Sophia Perennis
Translation © Friends in Spirit 2024
Series Editor: James R. Wetmore

All rights reserved

No part of this book may be reproduced or transmitted,
in any form or by any means, without permission

For information, address:
Friends in Spirit
Box 931, Philmont, NY 12565

ISBN 978-1-59731-234-9 (pbk)
ISBN 978-1-59731-235-6 (cloth)

Cover Design: Michael Schrauzer

CONTENTS

Biographical Sketch i
Foreword 1
Preface 4
Self-Knowledge 11
Laziness 13
Misplaced Desires 15
Incivility 17
The Precursor 19
Waste 21
Reversals of Fortune 23
Apathy 25
The Virgin 27
Marital Quarrels 29
Sorrows of the Heart 31
Familiarity 33
Christ 35
Liberty and Fate 37
The Motives Behind our Acts 39
Peace of Heart 41
The Mission of Jesus 43

Compassion 45
Vengeance 47
Feverish Haste 49
The Temptations of Christ 51
Greed 53
In Search of Praise 55
Desire for Show 57
The Teachings of Christ 59
Slander 61
Falsehood 63
Calumny 65
The Miracles of Jesus 67
Misanthropy 69
Disgust with Life 71
Despair 73
The Transfiguration 75
Heedlessness 77
Obstinacy 79
Anxiety 81
The Last Supper 83
Prayer 85
Charity 87
Humility 89

The Death and Resurrection of Jesus   91
Illness   93
Mourning   95
The Fear of Death   97
The Ascension   99
Contempt   101
Criticism   103
Impatience   105
Apparitions of Christ After His Death   107
Melancholy   109
Insubordination   111
Perfection   113

Acknowledgments

The publisher is deeply indebted to the "friends" of *Les Amitiés Spirituelles*, who have kept Paul Sédir's books in print in French for over a century, and for the dedication of those who have nurtured the vision that one day these books might appear in worthy editions for Anglophone readers. We gratefully thank in this connection Piers Vaughn and Peter Urbanski for the exchange of textual materials many years ago that led to this presents series, Robert Ledwidge for his technical assistance, and especially Madame Zadah Guérin-McCaffery, who nurtured this same vision and worked towards its realization for decades. Her skilled devotion to Sédir's works helped ensure that Sédir's carefully crafted style has been preserved in these Friends in Spirit translations.

†

Biographical Sketch

Yvon le loup, son of Hippolyte Le Loup and Séraphine Foeller, was born on January 2, 1871 in Dinan, in the Côtes du Nord region of France. As a child, Yvon suffered the effects of tuberculosis, partial blindness, and a grave leg fracture that troubled him throughout his life. His mother, of Hessian origin, taught him German, which he later spoke fluently. At the age of nine, he made his First Communion at St Augustin's church, then entered the Jesuit school on rue des Francs Bourgeois, where he quickly distinguished himself by his great intelligence. Observant to a fault, he became a fine draughtsman and would have liked to paint. He was drawn to music, drawing, literature, and was extraordinarily dexterous with his hands. In due course, however, he was obliged to pursue a more practical academic course, owing to the influence of his father, an old soldier imbued with discipline who had little understanding for the refinement of this quiet child with lofty aspirations. And so, as soon a Yvon passed his academic exams (1892), he joined the Banque de France. He was twenty-one years old.

A few years earlier, in his late teens (around 1890), a profound shift in Yvon's orientation had taken shape. Not far from the Banque de France was an esoteric bookshop and publishing house (La Librairie du Merveilleux), where Yvon soon met the well-known writer on esoteric matters, Dr. Gerard Encausse (Papus). This led to a great friendship between the two quite different men. Papus set the young Yvon to work organizing his extensive esoteric library and introduced him to numerous personalities from the heady, even feverish, esoteric milieu of the time. One evening, he was taken to the home of Stanislas de Guaita, a nobleman of Italian descent who possessed the most complete esoteric library then in existence. Around this time, Yvon published an article ("An Experiment in Practical Occultism") and made his debut as a speaker on the theme: "Divinatory Sciences and Chiromancy."

In 1891, Papus had formed the Order of Martinists, based on the teachings of "The Unknown Philosopher," Louis Claude de Saint-Martin (1743–1803), and asked Yvon to collaborate. This fraternity took up the ideas of Martinez de Pasqually's Kabbalistic rite, and formed the first initiatory level of Guaita's Rosicrucian fraternity. In these circles, young authors frequently used pseudonyms. Yvon took the name Paul Sédir (anagram of désir), Gerard Encausse became Papus, Dr. Emmanuel Lalande used the name Marc Haven, etc. From the time of his association with the new Martinist Order, Yvon regularly published his work as Paul Sédir.

In 1895, Papus passed his doctorate in medicine and opened a home for the aged. This necessitated Sédir taking on the bulk of the esoteric-hermetic activities on which he and Papus had been collaborating. Every evening he gave classes in Hebrew and Sanskrit, the psychic training of Hindu fakirs, yoga, experimental alchemy, astrology, esoteric botany, etc. He also organized various research groups on related subjects.

Biographical Sketch

Sédir was also much attracted to mysticism, and frequented literary circles such that of the poet Paul-Marie Verlaine. Meanwhile, in the rue de l'Ancienne Comédie, meetings of the Martinist Order were taking place, where Sédir became acquainted with individuals engaged in experiments regarding which he would later say: "It is here-below that you pay the highest price." His alchemical research did, however, enable him to acquire an ever deeper understanding of the foundations of what is known as the Great Work.

All these early aspects of Sédir's esoteric life reveal an overarching quest for truth that always led him to first experience something before speaking about it. He had by now attained great heights of "secret" knowledge, and even power. But to his great good fortune he had the wisdom to detach himself from these as soon as he realized their worthlessness and danger.

In July 1897, Gerard Encausse arranged for Sédir (then 26 years old) to meet a most singular man, Master Philippe of Lyon (Nizier Anthelme Philippe), to whom he was introduced by Madame Encausse. Master Philippe was a remarkable healer whom Sédir and others in his circle considered a Christian Master of the highest degree. Shortly after this meeting, Sédir left for Lyon to spend his vacation there. Just what happened at that time remains a private matter, although Sédir gives some inkling of what transpired in his autobiographical book *Initiations*, and also in a remarkable letter of May 1910:

> Together with some companions, I have done the rounds of all esotericisms and explored all crypts with

Weekly Meditations

the most fervent sincerity and hope of success. But none of the certainties I eventually grasped appeared to be The Certainty. Rabbis communicated their secret manuscripts to me; alchemists admitted me to their laboratories; Sufis, Buddhists, and Taoists led me during long nights to the abodes of their gods; a Brahmin let me copy his tables of mantra; a yogi imparted to me the secrets of contemplation. But one evening, after a certain meeting, what these admirable men taught became for me like haze rising at dusk on a sultry day. We run after what we think is hidden, but know nothing of our own religion, though its dogma and liturgy are the most complete presentation of integral knowledge on earth. Everything is there in Christianity. The Hindu *trimurti* is neither the Christian trinity nor the Pythagorean ternary; gnosis and the gospels do not lead to the same goal. Read in the texts what is there, not what one would wish to find there. To see that we know nothing; to experience that we can do nothing; to verify that heaven is here within us, and that our Friend constantly enfolds us within his blessed arms—this is the lesson of Jesus. This I have attempted to say by publishing, among other works, five volumes of lectures on the gospels.

Master Philippe had changed Sédir's orientation. *His mission had been affirmed.* He gave up all the esoteric fraternities (and his various ranks and offices in them) in order to devote himself wholly to living and spreading the gospel. His commentaries on the life of Christ are especially notable in that he accepts the intuitive faculty as a means of approaching the Truth. Sédir's literary output was extensive. His best known works are from this period are: *Prayer,*

Biographical Sketch

Initiations, Mystic Forces, Christian Mysticism, Seven Mystical Gardens, The Childhood of Jesus, The Sermon on the Mount, Some Friends of God, The Healings of Christ, The Kingdom of God, The Crowning of His Work, Weekly Meditations, and *The Incandescent Path.* His lectures and books drew many devoted students, and in due course a fellowship called Les Amitiés Spirituelles ("Friends in Spirit") was formed. This organization undertook to publish many of Sédir's books, and though it is much diminished, it remains active today.

Sédir died in Paris. Twenty years later, Breton poet and novelist Théophile Briant of Dinan wrote:

> On February 3, 1926, Paul Sédir died in Paris at the age of 55. The death of this admirable man, with his gospel-inspired heart, went almost unnoticed by the mainstream press, which was more preoccupied with crowning the charlatans and histrionics who were entertaining the public, even as international catastrophes were on the verge of breaking out. Apart from the chosen few whom this Apostle of the End Times had called to the Light, most post-war jabberers were unaware that one of the century's most eloquent voices was no longer to be heard. His was a forerunner's voice, the voice of a herald proclaiming in a wilderness of contentious crowds, a voice that had been devoted for years to spreading the gospel and, at the threshold of the abyss, was raised in dire warning against the multiplied prostitutions of the word.†

---

† This sketch is based on biographical materials provided by Émile Besson and Max Camis (close friends of Sédir), recently published in English in *Paul Sédir: His Life and Work* (Friends in Spirit, 2024).

Foreword

THE BASIC PRINCIPLE of our progress lies neither in our intelligence nor in our instinct, but in our feeling soul—in our spiritual heart that sheathes the inmost sanctuary of the self—the volatile core of will where the ray of our eternal soul comes to a focus. Our soul life manifests itself through the passions, which narrow down to love and hate. In spite of what some Eastern asceticisms may teach, these must not be destroyed, for anything is preferable to inertia. We must uproot them from the soil of selfishness. They must be sublimated, transmuted, and restored to their supernatural state in God—in pure Love. This may be attained only through an effective imitation of the Word, Jesus. We must sculpt ourselves into the likeness of this model: our eyes ever focused upon Him, our hands ceaselessly working for Him.

Every book on religious exercises could be entitled "Imitations of Jesus Christ." May I be forgiven for having written another. I have made it as short as possible, and only in obedience to the wishes of my most indulgent friends. The way of using it is as follows. Each morning, after our first prayer, let us immerse ourselves in the supernatural unknowing of faith and ask God again for His Truth. Then, let us read one of these pages carefully, ardently, in deepest inner silence. Let these readings quickly become contemplations. Let the

Weekly Meditations

heart replace intelligence. Let us try to love instead of trying to understand. Then let us pledge ourselves to practice the observance with which each meditation ends. Finally, we should rapidly plan our day. The whole exercise should take no more than fifteen minutes. For the life of the true disciple is active, not contemplative; practical, not theoretical. These themes are arranged in groups of four. In each series there is a meditation upon one aspect of Christ's life (Nos. 1, 5, 9, 13, etc.) that is commented upon by the three succeeding meditations on the moral life of the disciple—these three relating to the first. Thus a partial synthesis may be realized every four weeks. Later on, a Friend will probably be able to transform this rough draft into a complete manual for every day of the year. This will be done easily by condensing the Gospels of the Evangelists, just as Catholic liturgy does, and dividing them among the well-known periods, such as:

The Preparation for the Birth of the Word within us (Advent)
Mystical Christmas
Epiphany
The Childhood of Christ
The Mission of Christ (Ash Wednesday, Lent)
The Passion (Holy Week), Easter (Resurrection, Emmaus)
Ascension, Pentecost (Whitsuntide)
Assumption
The Apostolic life of the disciple
The permanent and invisible Life of the Master
All Saints' Day

Foreword

Obviously, this little book does not take the place of prayer or of charitable acts. Neither does it take the place of resisting temptations or the advice of enlightened men. We offer here but one path among others. Nonetheless, since its intensive use will give us self-knowledge, and since the greatest obstacle to our perfection is ourselves, this path may become efficacious, and perhaps even surpass our hopes.

†

Preface

"Watch, for you know neither the day nor
the hour when the bridegroom will appear."
(Matthew 25:13)

THE PARABLE of the Five Wise Virgins and the Five Foolish Virgins recurs every day. So let us be attentive to our acts. Do we not see our indolence, our inattention to God? Are we not aware of the vivacity of our selfishness? Do we not see among us the inoperative Platonism of our friendships: rigidity preventing our souls from fusing with each other; aloofness rendering us incapable of exaltation through one another? Are we not aware of the reason why we are so unsuccessful in comforting the weary and shaking the indifferent out of their lethargy? It is because we are still immersed in vacuity, too preoccupied with the unreality of our personal problems, too submerged in our petty covetousness. We must at all costs and with decisive purpose free ourselves. Otherwise, rough shepherds will someday prod us forward with spears instead of crooks. To watch, to remain awake, to be vigilant by overcoming somnolence, lethargy, and emptiness of soul—that is what the Master recommends to us. Let us not close the eyes of our spirit before ugliness, before beauty, before the excitement of pleasures or sorrows. We must be aware of everything. There is no investigation or analysis that demands

Preface

from the scientist as much precision, freedom, and honesty, as the Christian needs in his analysis of self and of the world.

We must be aware of all that happens in the partial sphere psychology calls the conscious. We must weigh everything therein according to evangelical law. In that sphere we must become tyrants of the self. But once we have reconstructed our personality in the likeness of Jesus (at least insofar as we can perceive Him), let us give free rein to our enthusiasm in order to call with all our might—which discipline will have increased tenfold the unknown form (so much more beautiful, true, and lofty) of Him Who is waiting only for our cry for help, to come down to us. To join the Lord is such a simple thing; it is so simple that we must make numerous attempts before discovering the means.

Let us constantly return to basic principles. First, we must acquire the greatest power of attention, and then invincible perseverance. We must also acquire such inner freedom as makes us incapable of regrets no matter what difficulties we may have encountered in obtaining results—even when we are denied the fruits of those efforts. Finally, we must have the calm courage that fears nothing.

All of this may be summed up in one word, patience: the strength to accept, the strength to suffer. Perfect patience consecrates us kings of ourselves. That is why many have cried out: let us either suffer, or die! If we could only see the future of splendor that suffering prepares for us, how we would welcome this harsh visitor, how we would seek it out and hold on to it with rapture.

But I cannot constrain anyone to this mystical gesture that only a few accomplish, to this embracing of the Cross, to this secret conflagration. I may not even ask our Friend to "incline" you towards it. You are free. You must choose and start of your own accord. I can only repeat: Truth, Reality, Life are to be found therein.

I am well aware that we are slumbering in the night, but at least may the unique star of faith illumine our night, may it be perfumed with the great breaths of Love. Joy is not to be found in things. Rather, we will find it in our heart after having emptied its powerlessness and cinders into the incandescent heart of our Master, Who alone loves us everlastingly.

We are weak only to the extent that we rely upon ourselves. We are lukewarm only if we fail to feed our fire. We are fearful only when we find ourselves alone. So let us lean upon Him Who is Strength. Let us burn our selfishness. Let us cling to the mantle of the Good Shepherd: He is never happier than when we importune Him.

As our body experiences weariness, so does our spirit. These slack periods are to be expected. They are almost inevitable, although we should try to shorten their duration and reduce our indolence to a minimum. Lukewarmness usually results from habitually neglecting small duties—which is dangerous because of its apparent harmlessness. When we cease to ascend the narrow path, it is because we are sliding backward towards the precipice. It is written: "Would to God that thou wert completely cold." And also: "I will vomit the lukewarm from my mouth." Saint Bernard thought the conversion of a criminal easier than that of a tepid monk.

We must force ourselves to meticulously fulfill our duties. Those who overlook little faults will fall into bigger ones. We must also force ourselves to pray at every oppor-

Preface

tune moment, even when we do not feel inclined to do so. If, while praying, we are distracted and not duly concerned about the distraction; if we are disgusted and are curt towards someone; if we do not give sufficient time to our duties; if we commit faults and no longer care; if we read just to kill time; if we take our ease or work only to evade being noticed—all of that adds up to lukewarm indifference. And the remedy for it is action.

We must act with pure intentions. For God, for our brothers, act with exactitude, calm, and orderliness. Act with fervor, without negligence. Act with courage, even if our work holds no interest for us. Act with perseverance, and never leave work unfinished. It is not via the intellect that we act, it is by our feelings, through passion, through our animic center; in a word: through love. The will is but a phase of love: whether it springs from instinct, whether it robes itself in the sumptuous folds of intelligence, whether it hides under the shield of pride—the essential principle of the will remains Love.

Love needs but itself in order to expand, for the more love gives, the stronger it becomes, and the more magnificent is its rebirth. Love is not concerned with probabilities for success. It ignores prudent vacillation, skillful stratagems, timid precautions. When once love sees a tear, it hastens to wipe it away. Love offers itself between aggressor and victim, and though weak, denuded, and without defenses, love triumphs and overcomes all violence. Its power resides in its spontaneity—for at root, Love is identical with the Spirit. Love, fervor, fire: that is what we should pray for daily, from morning till night.

Almost everything is possible for one who wills; everything is possible for one who loves. But we must be all love, we must love constantly—and each hour a little more than the hour before. We must ceaselessly evoke in ourselves the sensitive aspect of God, which is Love. We must force ourselves to love. When our sensitivity recoils before certain physical and moral horrors, we must force ourselves to perform the gestures of human and divine brotherhood. Many anemic souls claim they are not capable of such efforts. They expect everything from Heaven. This is a mistake. "God helps those who help themselves." Energy is essential—disciplined, systematic energy. Our nature must be tamed, then trained all the more, in the manner of a police dog. Otherwise our impulsivity would merely incite discouraging failures. We will be able to yield to our enthusiasms once our training has been perfected, because henceforth they will soar towards Jesus only.

But, may I repeat that, first, we must undergo a preparation, a cleansing, and purification. Preparation is by the desire we all have to do good. The needed cleansing is our corporal, moral, and mental discipline. Purification means accepting trials that, coming from the inferior worlds, are conveyed to us by the agents of destiny at a slower or faster pace according to our goodwill and to our power of resistance. Purification also includes the invisible work of the angels of Jesus upon our cold and hardened heart in order to soften it and set it ablaze.

The pages you are going to read in this short book are related to the second of these three stages, the one which consists entirely in the training of the self. Primarily, we must obey the maxims of renunciation in the strictest sense of the word. Each time we are about to do something that is clearly neither a duty nor a charitable act (were it even the most insignificant thing in the world), each time a

Preface

thoughtless impulse not born out of devotion springs up in us, we must curb it and force ourselves to perform the opposite act. Our Jesus condemned Himself to a whole life of sensations, of works, and of unbearable overcrowding with the exquisite fineness and subtlety of His nature. Therefore, let us constrain ourselves. Let us never give in to the self. Let us feed the self generously with that which it does not like. In the face of each acquisition, of each experience, and of each delight life offers us, let us first ask ourselves: "Do I like this, would I do it gladly?" If the answer is "yes," let us refuse, and take the opposite stand. After partaking from these bitter cups to the dregs, our spirit will be assuaged and enlightened. At the same time it will become capable of reaching a larger number of spirits. From then on we will be bathed in the pure light of Love, we will no longer need syllogisms in order to arrive at actions. True life will be within us. When facing any creature, or in face of any event, our intelligence will immediately understand, our heart will be suddenly moved, and our arms will automatically reach out to relieve the burden of the weak. Eminent feats of heroism are not the most difficult. On the contrary, little sacrifices are by far the finest. They are the minute crystals that amalgamate to form the imperishable walls of the Divine City when burnt by the billions at the hearth of Love.

Mystical asceticism is the admirable common denominator here. All you need do is focus your thoughts upon Jesus for both your most ordinary tasks and your furthest preoccupations in order that you may unite them towards that final goal which is both so near and yet so far. If you can remember that among all the worlds populated with responsible and intelligent beings, this Earth is included

Weekly Meditations

among the small number that up till now have welcomed the Manifest Word upon them, you will understand why those who are willing victims can also make themselves heard by the One Who is the Word of the Father.

The themes I offer you in this manual are intended to offer a breathing spell in the midst of the fight—to realize ourselves, to be reminded of the principles, to concentrate our attention, and to reinforce our personal contact with our Master. These themes are only examples. You may choose others. The main point is that the disciple may relax his mind occasionally, thanks to which he will realize his powers with more assurance, lucidity, and calm; so that he might prepare himself to lead to the labor of mystical service the sum-total of the energies of his reason, body, and heart, welded together in total harmony. The magnificent result of this threefold discipline will be the oneness of our being.

†

Self-Knowledge

"Who is it you are looking for?"
(John 18:4)

JESUS IS HERE, silently. He stands at the door of my heart. He is waiting. I have just discovered that ambitions, passions, and pleasures are mere ashes. Jesus is here. His eyes, which pierce all things, are cast downward, lest the penetration of His glance might intimidate me. He keeps silent, lest His voice might overwhelm me. He keeps His merciful Hands hidden, lest their contact would ignite the conflagration of Love in my blood, too soon.

He waits because He wants the whole of me: from my body (built by His ministers) to my heart (where His angels are erecting His sanctuary). He waits, for He does not want to take me; He wants me to give myself. His tenderness desires only what I offer Him. It is with a view to this gesture on my part that He has placed quagmires and mirages on my path. Since I did not want to believe Him, I must undergo my tests. Weariness and fear will turn me to Him. I did not want to listen to Him. Just as a beast throws himself into the river, so, some night, maddened by remorse, I will plunge into the irresistible currents of Love.

Grant that I may explore my inner deserts to their innermost recesses. That I may grasp all ghosts, taste all fruits. That I might convince myself there is a universal mirage, in order that I will not expect anything from anyone, save from God.

May this period of waiting be active, not inert. May it be filled with my inmost supplications, with the sorrows of my spirit, by its disquietude, its hastiness, its anxieties, its precipitations... until such time as, having prepared within myself a neat chamber and having embellished it with the flowers of charitable acts, the Angel can sing there hymns of thanksgiving and swing the censer of adoration therein, so that at last the Lord Himself will descend therein for the definitive birth that will bring me to the threshold of Eternity.

Observance: Each evening let me make a short but thorough examination of my conscience.

Laziness

*"As for the unprofitable servant,
cast him into the darkness without."*
(Matthew 25:30)

THERE IS A deep-rooted laziness that prevents even the pursuit of pleasure. Then again, there is a more common laziness that simply desires to avoid tedious tasks. The first is almost incurable. The second can be cured. Many are compelled to perform mechanical and tedious labors that crush their vitality. Doubtless, they are in a manner convicts or slaves, but is not the one who considers himself free really a slave? And, might I not be just such a madman?

However, since I know that any work can be profitable to me, are my aversions in this regard justifiable? When I consider a task unworthy of me, might it not be, rather, that I misunderstand its significance? Did I really want to raise that task up to be my dream? If not, then I must try something new. If I have neither this boldness nor this confidence, I deprive myself of the right to complain. To complain is to weaken oneself. Consequently I will have to follow the school of resignation.

Am I too vain to accept the dreary, humdrum events of everyday life without a murmur? To overcome bad luck, I must overcome myself. And You, Christ my Lord, You

Weekly Meditations

builder of the worlds, You have worked with carpenters' tools. You Who feed the universe, You have sat at table with men. You Who knew all things, with what patience have You not listened and do still listen to our prattling? You, Who possess all and need nothing, have You not come down and have you not toiled? Are You not still doing over and over, unceasingly, the same endless labor to which our rebellious will constrains Your love?

Observance: I must fight against all forms of inertia, both inside and outside myself.

Misplaced Desires

"Jesus replied: 'You do not know what it is that you ask.'"
(Matthew 20:22)

THE LAW does not censure the motives that impel my actions in search of beauty, glory, or knowledge. However, I realize there are motives of greater purity. The "gods" have many a worshipper, God but a few. How many times have I sought a demigod, even a devil, while believing and saying that my sole concern was with the Savior Himself? But that is not a mortal sin. Pursuing a shadow is still pursuing something, and God Who is Life wants me to live. Grant that I do not fall prey to my illusions any longer. Grant that I may see clearly within myself! Grant that the Spirit may dart His dazzling Splendor upon me!

What a man he could be who alloys Eastern patience with American initiative when conducting his business, and yet who cares nothing for his acquired millions! What a scientist he would be who recognizes his own ignorance! What a leader he would be who devotes his mind and sensitivity to working for the benefit of the lowest of primitives!

To become indifferent to the result of any act after having been passionately concerned for its success would be an insoluble antinomy, were it not for the dormant little flame that comes ablaze at the mere passage of the Breath of God inside of me. Not money, power, renown, love, art, or thought will ever light that lamp, because they are but mere reflections. This flame is the original one—self-subsistent, inextinguishable, victorious. It is gentleness itself, before which all conflagrations abate. It gives forth light and warmth without burning. The heart of the blackest archangel bursts and melts beneath its mysterious radiance.

I will tend this lamp in the most secret chamber of my self. It will give me humility. That it may cast its light all around, I will carry this lamp, holding it aloft to the brows, lowering it over the mires—and this will be charity. Thus my desires for the perishable will die in order that they may be reborn into the Imperishable.

Observance: Never satisfy any personal desire.

Incivility

"When you enter into a house, you are to wish it well."
(Matthew 10:12)

I AM RIGHT to remain courteous towards an ungracious person, but it would be still better were I to dispel my irritation. I would then be sincerely courteous, and my courteousness would carry with it the fruits of sincerity. If I am polite only to make a good impression, I pay homage to the gods of worldly opinion, of falsehood, and of vanity.

Rudeness is only the defense reflex of my selfishness, lethargy, and whims. When I am deeply engrossed in thought over some important matter and an unexpected caller bursts into my office, or if a loiterer stops me in the street, why should I grow impatient? These people, like me, are moving signs of the cosmic force, and so may have something to tell me even without their being aware of it. And maybe, even if I have not understood their secret message, they will have made me stronger and better since, thanks to them, I will have mastered my nerves and taken a step towards sincerity; and also, by my having been amiable to them, perhaps they will have remembered that kindness does exist. No, these small things are neither ridiculous nor to be scorned. This whole earth is made up of infinitely small things.

I practice to perfect myself to the extent that my weakness permits me to do so. It is up to me to enrich my inner life with such pure splendors and such lofty sumptuousness that my outer life will then become incapable of pettiness. By dint of accumulating the grains of sand of my little virtues into a heap, I will finally succeed in cementing the foundations of my Temple.

Observance: Grant that my Ideal suffuse my face, my person, my words, even my bearing and gestures!

✝

The Precursor

"John appeared in the wilderness."
(Mark 1:4)

THE PRECURSOR is as mysterious as his Master. Son of the elderly, longtime barren, and repentant Elizabeth, and of Zecharias, the old man athirst for God, he represents my purified self. He is the fulfillment of divine promise. He is the first among men. He represents abstinence. He is naked. He is filled with the Spirit. He walks straight ahead. He cries in the wilderness. He is terrible, yet he draws me to him. Compared to him I feel as a clod of earth at the base of a mountain. Yet he does not frighten me. Something tells me that he too has been a clod of earth, and that I—if I want (if I will it!)—I too someday will reach the height of that gigantic peak. That is, if I will! If I will to do everything necessary for that end. If I will as I should.

Oh yes, I fathom and understand quite well that Ram, Fo-Hi, Sesostris, Plato, Caesar, Marcus Aurelius, St Augustine, Charlemagne, Shakespeare, Napoleon, and all other illustrious men, can none of them measure up to the Precursor. If it is true that he has indeed preceded the Word on all His paths, if it is really he who walks before the Word on all His paths, if he has the right of calling all men to repentance—he must be, then, the formidable Athlete of God, one of the Knights of the Spirit, one of the perpetual Witnesses.

My thoughts, unaccustomed to spiritual grandeurs, stops short here. It is now up to my soul to continue the journey. My logic falters. May my admiration leap forward so as to open a gap to Love! May the austerity of the Great Penitent teach me to be hard with myself. May the martyrdom and weariness he faced teach me to become tender and compassionate towards others. May his isolation teach me to love solitude. May his independence make me cherish sincerity.

Observance: Let me deliberately deprive myself each day of some enjoyment, so that I may learn how to become humble.

✝

Waste

"If he is poor, even what he accounts
his own will be taken from him."
(Matthew 25:29)

Do I ever consider how much labor, how may failed attempts, how much ingenuity is spent to manufacture the thousand little things I waste everyday? How much energy expended so that I may toast a slice of bread, button a garment, write a letter? Could I but recapitulate each evening how many useless gestures I have made, how many useless words I have uttered, how many objects were thrown away, how much food wasted, how many needless steps taken, how much aimless musing and powers wasted through caprice or by idleness! Nevertheless, I am aware that Nature keeps account of everything—of a bruised leaf just as much as of an eye-wink prompted by vanity. I know that I am her debtor and that when I misuse her loans, leaving them unproductive, or when I dissipate them, I contract a similar responsibility. He who throws bread in the gutter condemns himself to ruin. He who without a valid motive wastes his strength or intelligence calls down upon himself imbecility and weakness.

I will mitigate the results of my heedlessness only by learning how to control myself, by doing everything at the right time (recalling how precious is time). I am an integral part of a great and compact whole. The invisible binds me to every creature much more securely than vitality holds together the organs of the body and their cells. None of the energies I expend are ever lost. Nothing put within my reach, seemingly by chance, is ever without value.

Observance: Let me be thrifty towards myself and generous towards others.

Reversals of Fortune

"It is easier for a camel to go through the eye of a
needle than for a rich man to enter the Kingdom of God."
(Mark 10:25)

WEALTH IS A favor from the Genius of the Earth. From God's standpoint it is a test—one of the hardest. To lose it would mean being relieved of cumbersome baggage. Nevertheless, the parables of the Gospel tell us that the rich men must not try to escape the responsibilities of their status, nor immobilize their wealth either through fear or by distaste of effort. A millionaire need not change his status. It is preferable that each one keeps his position according to social or worldly customs. In any case, a really charitable and wealthy family does not hoard—quite to the contrary. And why should we not "ruin ourselves" for noble motives, given that many ruin themselves so easily for shameful ones?

If I am ruined through my own fault, I have only to start again with courage and repentance. If I have been ruined through my idealism or charity, peace of heart comforts me. If the ruin occurred through unlucky circumstances, I know that misfortune is a powerful tonic. When gold is flowing, do we not believe it is on account of our own cleverness? Do we not view our profitable acumen with rather too much indulgence? And do we not despise the unlucky?

Weekly Meditations

Each of us almost always works according to a providential design without being aware of, and almost always without "willing" it—regardless whether we are a bungling failure or the most grasping of business tycoons. There will always be poor people and rich people, until such time as men have learned to love one another. A millionaire can be "poor in spirit": if he acknowledges himself merely the manager of his wealth, he is closer to Truth than the spiteful, crafty beggar.

Observance: I must never refuse to render a service to anyone by using the pretext that my purse is empty.

†

Apathy

"The Kingdom of Heaven has opened to force,
and the forceful take it by storm."
(Matthew 11:12)

DURING DULL periods when I have no great desires, when my energy is somnolent, when I have not the strength even to despair, the masters of inner life unanimously teach that I must not allow this state of being to overly concern me. I know that in a solar system, while a certain number of planets are active, some others are in repose. The whole man is a solar system in which the earthly man, the terrestrial part of him, is but a planet.

Then, again, it is God Whom I seek. If indeed He is the Universe, the Supreme, the Perfect, how can I who am imperfect in essence ever grasp Him? Surely, not unless there occurs in my nature a change called regeneration. Every time I feel God inside me, it is because He has adapted His greatness to my littleness. And when I no longer feel Him, when there remains in me nothing but a distant remembrance of Him, it is because He is approaching me under a new aspect, with a greater power. It is just during these periods of apathy that I must exert the most intense effort, that I must cling to Him, that I must wring from the depths of my being the supreme cry of an obstinate faith affirming itself against any evidence to the contrary.

May this passing somnolence not prevent me from fulfilling my daily tasks. When everything sickens me, seeming insipid and dull, I must conceal my disgust and go right on living like anyone else—that is the most perfect act.

Suffering is inconsequential when I am filled with enthusiasm. But to suffer is difficult when I am sad, when I am devoid of hope and courage. Still, that is what I must do. This I will achieve through the all-powerful strength of humility, through the infinite weakness of my nothingness.

Observance: Love everyone and everything in a practical manner.

✝

The Virgin

"Behold the Handmaid of the Lord."
(Luke 1:38)

IF THE ENVOYS of the spirit can be recognized by the hatred they provoke, the Virgin certainly belongs to their cohort, for tradition teaches that few women have been as humiliated, misunderstood, scorned, or treated with contempt, as has she.

The Virgin is the first expression by which God chose to indicate the nobility of woman and her role. There was nothing noticeable outwardly about this unexplainable figure whose soul was the altar of the greatest sacrifices and the sanctuary of the greatest mysteries. As a child she was brought up in a cloistered setting. During adolescence she was burdened with the duties of an indigent household and the challenges of bringing up the most delicate of beings. As a mother she was for thirty-three years martyred through the daily anxieties and frightful anguish of an already apprehended future. As an obscure widow without resources she nevertheless managed the suffering little community of disciples. Truly, the wife of Joseph is living proof that a life spent in the shadows often veils the most meritorious of works.

A hero conquers admiration when a sudden crisis raises him up above his norm and enables him to perform a heroic deed. But the most difficult deed is to forget oneself, coldly, reasonably, systematically, through all the small duties of the household, the workshop, or the street. The imitation of Christ is impossible for our human nature left to its own resources. But the imitation of the Virgin is possible. Mary is closer to our wretched souls, and more commiserating with the tribulations of our everyday life.

I am well aware that the figure of the Virgin is to be found in a great many other religions, in symbolism, and hermeneutics. But these are too often multifaceted adornments prone to stimulate the intellect and perceptions. But for us, since actions alone count, during our periods of lassitude we will focus wholly on evoking the precarious existence of the Mother of Christ—who seen from without appears silent and hidden, but seen from within is ardent and dazzling.

Observance: Never complain.

†

Marital Quarrels

"And so they are no longer two, they are one flesh; what God then has joined, let no man put asunder."
(Matthew 19:6)

How many dissertations on matters of marriage or celibacy doze on library shelves! Seen from above, the problem is quite simple: our primary task here-below is to become kind. Will it be easier for me to learn kindness in the marriage state or outside of it? The answer remains a personal one.

Married life should be the school of true Love. It alone furnishes to my aspirations the necessary tribulations found in daily living. It alone keeps me from dangerous experiences and unworthy capitulations. Marriage brings the phantasmagorias of youthful dreams to a focus, frees them from shadowy veils, and changes them into living, constant lights.

As the saying goes, no man is a great hero to his valet. Just as rare are the old couples who still have for each other the admiring fervor of the engagement period. How much care must a husband or a wife deploy to remain worthy of each other's mutual choice! What a masterpiece is the marriage that keeps intact the beauties of the first months until death parts them! A combination of intelligence, will, and delicate attentions will be sorely needed!

Married life alone teaches mutual service and abnegation in the small things that serve as pedestal to the bigger ones. Married couples are at work on a masterpiece bigger than they are, and worth more to them, as well as to others, than any other exceptional effort. No dissension, no dissonance should affect that union. Even the serious faults of either husband or wife should be used and serve to render their union indestructible. Remember: marriage alone tests our patience, our tenderness, the inalterable serenity, the kindness full of grace, and all those generous forgivings of the Infinite that prove to be the various stages on the road to Heaven.

Observance: May each marriage partner apply himself or herself thoroughly, by every means that is not evil, to give happiness to the other.

✝

Sorrows of the Heart

"Abide then in my love."
(John 15:9)

LOVE BECOMES the most illusory of mirages if what I am seeking to find in it is my own image. If what I try to find in the person I love most is nothing but an echo of myself, this kind of love is only a search for pleasure or for sentimental selfishness. Love becomes the stablest of realities only when I use it as a fervor of sacrifice.

Most loves are only charismatic fascinations. We know so little about these mysterious forces. That is why passions are often disconcerting to the spectator and why their psychology almost always remains speculative. As we are incapable of giving ourselves to others through duty, Nature pours us a magic draught. This volatile inebriation, hurling us from exaltation to bitterness, from frenzy to disgust, does however at least instruct us in the elementary gestures of altruism—or rather, it impels us into performing them.

There is no single precedent disproving that two lovers, no matter how well matched they may be, will not sooner or later be obliged to sacrifice some preferences or some comforts for each other. Moreover, the sum-total of such annoyances will quickly exceed the sum-total of their joys. But even more than debauchery, more than passion, what poisons in us our power to love, what dries up our inmost and deepest springs, is that perversity of breach of faith and deceit in which many glory with a miserable pride.

That a man should covet a woman is a weakness, a lack of restraint. But when he feels no compunction in stealing another man's wife, in breaking up a home, in dissolving a contract that had been freely entered into previously—that is a grievous matter indeed. It condemns him, it enchains him for perhaps several centuries of that life beyond the grave, the duration of which remains forever an "unknown quantity" to us here-below.

Furthermore, marriages are inscribed in Heaven from the very beginning. Except with marriage in view then, no man should desire a woman, nor woman let herself be seduced.

Observance: When those one I love make me suffer, let me try to love them for themselves—in God, forgetting myself.

✝

Familiarity

*"It was I Who chose you, that you should
go out and bring forth fruit…"*
(John 15:16)

WHEN I RESENT the rather overwhelming exuberance of certain people, I am willing to use a more distant approach towards them and, if need be, season my politeness with a barb or two. But am I justified in this? Had I kept my distance from such people under all circumstances, I would not have had to endure these invasive effusions—unless in actual truth my reserve stemmed from arrogance rather than from kindly discretion.

After all, have I also not at some time or other annoyed someone either through thoughtlessness, importunity, or vanity? There must be a just measure in all things. I must not shun my neighbors, any more than waste hours with them. I must not be timid or disdainful or a gossip. I must always maintain a certain detachment that keeps me sufficiently free from expecting anything from anyone. After all, from God's standpoint, no one owes me a thing!

I must ever be ready to sympathize with others so as to respond cordially to any tokens of affection they may give me—even if I hold those tokens to be banal or prompted by self-interest. Till now, I have probably almost always engaged with others with outward courtesy, while inwardly wondering what I could get from them. From this day on I must eradicate this calculation (even if involuntary) from my heart. I must greet all and sundry with a fraternal glance. I must strive to reverse this mute internal interrogation in such a way that it rises from my heart to my brain—so that I may think instead: How may I be of service to my brother?

Observance: Cordially welcome everyone; never impose upon anyone.

Christ

"You will find a babe wrapped in swaddling clothes, lying in a manger…"
(Luke 2:12)

AFTER OUR INTELLECT has exhausted every explanation regarding the mystery expressed in the above verse, it can do no other than declare itself powerless before this definition of the Infinite, this localization of the Universal, this particularization of the Perfect. No matter how vast or complex the intellect may imagine the Relative to be, there is an impassable abyss separating it from the Absolute. Ever since men have begun to think, they have always felt it impossible to grasp primordial Unity apart from a total annihilation of the self. Likewise, it will always be impossible for me to *understand* the Incarnation of the Word as long as I will be a creature in Creation. But I may come to *receive* this miracle—the miracle, that is, of the splendor of the humanized Word present in the holiness of my being.

The Word is born of the Father since *before* time. But then, one day *in* time, He was born in Bethlehem. And He can be born again in countless births in the souls of all who follow Him on this Earth and wheresoever else we humans may live. To believe that Jesus is the only Son of God made

Weekly Meditations

flesh is a gift awarded to anyone who recognizes his own, and total, nothingness. But it is only at a particular stage of our voyage through Existence that we each become capable of receiving that light. Another gift we may receive is that of feeling God being born in us. But for this we must first be sufficiently impoverished, denuded, and purified. That is, all temporal powers and things within us must first have made room for eternal powers and things.

To feel God living in us; to participate in His omnipotence, His omniscience; to be free because, having accepted the fetters for so long, we have finally worn them away; to offer the Father the supreme homage of this liberty finally won—then, by acting like Jesus, Son of Man; to us is revealed that He acted, living in the Father and the Father living in Him—this final form of our being, the only true one, is still a gift. To obtain these three privileges, there is but one lone thing to accomplish: the imitation of Our Lord Jesus Christ.

Observance: Covet nothing, not even spiritual favors.

☦

Liberty and Fate

"If the Son makes you free men, you shall be free indeed."
(John 8:36)

MADE FREE INDEED? Why? Because Jesus, Son of the Father, God Himself, equal to the Spirit, Master of the Spirit, is the only free one. Fate is the law of matter and the enigma of science. Liberty is the essence, the very manifestation of the spirit and the enigma of religion. These two forces coexist within us as the seeds of all other powers. They counterbalance each other alternatively therein. If we obey the self, then destiny—through atavism, habits, and influences of environment—will finally reduce us to complete slavery even while letting us believe we are free. But if we resist the self, though seemingly making ourselves a slave to it, we will become free.

Liberty has been promised us, but we must learn how to make use of it. What terrible power it is, in fact, *not* to find any obstacle to our desires! Individualism is a fight, a decomposition, a crumbling away, and the only true death. Slavery freely accepted, then, will be our road to liberty.

We need only look around us to notice that we become enslaved by obeying our passions. Close observation shows us that we will be still more enchained if we fight our passions only because of our pride to see ourselves surpass the crowds. In short, we must enter this battle only through love, through humility, in obedience to God, for His service, and to be useful to mankind. Then, and then only, will we escape the nets of destiny, from the coarsest to the least perceptible. Only then will our powers develop in directions other than those towards which anterior causes drove them, towards really new directions. Then, someday, our most glorious dreams will be surpassed.

Observance: I must accept the effort demanded by circumstances, especially if it particularly displeases me.

✝

The Motives Behind Our Acts

"Thy will be done on earth as it is in Heaven."
(Matthew 6:10)

THE FINAL WORD of all psychologies, the primary incentive of my acts, of my emotions, and of my thoughts is desire. In fact, my intelligence and my energy only get started under the impulse that in the final analysis comes from my "affective" center. Sensation, emotion, ideas are but secondary phenomena. Consequently, it will be the hidden motive that gives my acts their particular quality. Thus, a loafer wastes the same amount of energy hacking grass with his cane as the therapist expends in gathering healing herbs. The quality of energy output varies according to the motive.

I must then scrutinize my motives, discard all those not of the best moral caliber and choose among my goals the one that seems to be devoid of selfishness. Then and only then will my work be sound, harmonious, and alive. My being possesses but half of the answer to the riddle of life. The world holds the other half. They interpenetrate each other. Man is a little universe: a microcosm; the universe is the macrocosm: an immense man.

Any act is a holocaust sacrificed to an idol: be it fortune, glory, love, or science. The true God has but few, and rare, followers. In the final analysis, how many Christians are really nothing but idolaters! On the other hand, the concentration of a force increases it tenfold, or a hundredfold. Normally, I disperse my energies among the many daily tasks—but those are my natural forces or exterior faculties, which I can expand outwardly. I can, however, still retain in my innermost center my concentration and my unity. This is particularly so if I choose God as the basis or principle of all my motives and as the goal of all my works. From then on, having become one through spiritual Love (which is father to my desires) and multiple in my faculties, I will live in the image of the Absolute in an ever-increasing state of beatitude proportionate to my fervor.

Observance: Live only to serve God.

✝

Peace of Heart

"Peace is my bequest to you, I give you My peace."
(John 14:27)

To possess a force in such a way that it may become a constitutive part of my personality, I must bring it down from the summit of the spiritual heights where it exists in a state of perfection. And the sole and all-powerful evocation is the *act*. Hence I must act conformably with the ideal I expect to reach. If it is peace that I desire, I must eradicate all conflicts within myself and all battles around me. To possess concord, all discords must be made to vanish. To enjoy harmony, I must function harmoniously—all of which is contained in one word: forgiveness. Forgive all outer enemies, forgive all inner enemies. Forgive the former by offering them what they demand, and the latter by our perfect conformance to the law. To forgive evil does not mean to obey evil. If I alone am to suffer, I must submit to evil; but if others are being attacked by evil, I must prevent it.

La Fontaine, in his poems, which I read during my youth, showed me how the gigantic oak tree was felled by the same storm that the reed withstood. The smaller I become, the less envy I will provoke, and the more I will be at peace. However, this is only humility derived from fear and peace from selfishness. I must, rather, shrink the self on the one hand out of sincerity because I see myself as I am, contemptible and unworthy, and on the other out of love, in order to give to my brother for his various needs all that which is superfluous beyond my bare necessities. Whatever may happen to me through this unreasonable regimen, what have I to fear, since by so doing I imitate the infinite shrunkenness of Jesus, and since the Spirit blows where He wills?

Observance: I must work without seeking personal or selfish gain.

✝

The Mission of Jesus

*"I have come so that my sheep may have life
more abundantly . . . so that all those who believe
in me will not remain in darkness."*
(John 10:10; 12:46)

IF I DO NOT believe that Jesus is the only Son of God, I must then be accepting all the various human exegeses on offer: legends, solar myths, symbolisms, and initiations of Egypt, India, Chaldea, or of Tibet. But if even one particle of the meaning of divine things has been given to me, I who am so unworthy (because one always remains unworthy of receiving the smallest glimmer of Eternal Lights), I will indubitably know that Jesus has never been taught by any adept or by any god. Inversely to creatures, who evolve from below to above, He developed His terrestrial manifestation by proceeding from the inner to the outer. He involuted. Being the Way, the Life, and the Truth, He had no need of any instruction in order to know everything, no need of any kind of training to have all powers. He had only to be Himself.

Christ is a dual perfection: perfect Man and perfect God. He is not merely a man more advanced than others: He is the Man. He is not merely a god greater than the Brahmas, Ahura-Mazdas, or Jupiters: He is God. He is all the Powers of creatures, He is all the Powers of God: these are His robe and His mantle. Hence, from birth He knew all things and had command over all things. Only the expression of His knowledge or of His power was subjected to the laws of physiological growth—because He descended only to obey all these laws that He Himself had decreed from the beginning.

His gestures, His glance, and His words were sowing life. The soil, upon which He trod was receiving benediction from the contact of His feet. Moreover, each of these innumerable sparks from the divine that were left here and there in the dark mold of the world are awaiting the collaboration of my good will in order to rise and fructify. I too may become a gardener of these eternal flowers. Love is the supreme master.

Observance: Before performing any act, I must ask Jesus to illumine this act and its purpose.

†

Compassion

"Have pity on us and come to our succor."
(Mark 9:21)

THERE ARE three kinds of compassion. The first is an unhealthy sentimentality that reduces us to becoming the plaything of our nerves, the dupes of hypochondriacs, and the victims of our own deep-rooted vices. The second kind is found among those who, when ensconced in a comfortable armchair by the fireplace, exclaim: "How I pity those poor wretches who are going to sleep in freezing garrets tonight, and all those who huddle under bridges with an empty stomach!" The third kind of compassion—the only fruitful, real, and living one, is when, after having been moved by such thoughts, we grab our hat and go out on the street in search of such a wretch, to offer him a meal and a room. And if we do not have the money, it means bringing him—along with his filth and vermin—home with us to give him food and our bed.

Compassion means wasting my time, good-humoredly, at the bedside of a cranky invalid. It means not becoming angry when a poor man, hardened through misfortunes, insults and badgers me. It means finding comforting words for those who quite frankly seem to have earned their troubles, or for those who whine about any and everything. It means I will be indulgent, not with the surreptitious hope that others will be indulgent towards me someday, but because I am aware that, had I met the same temptation and had the same temperament, I may well have succumbed exactly as my neighbor did.

Whatever part of me is free from malevolence and contempt will give room to healthy reasoning, clear judgment, and indulgence. Thus it will be easier for me to find out how to remedy the sorrows of others. The more a man worries about himself, the smaller he becomes; the more he goes out of himself, the broader his view and the less assertive his power.

Observance: I must forbid myself the thought that any wretch or sick person suffers through his own fault.

†

Vengeance

> "Here is what I say to you who are listening to me:
> Love your enemies, do good to those who hate you;
> bless those who curse you, and pray for
> those who insult you."
> (Luke 6:27–28)

No one receives an insult or suffers hatred without having deserved it. Only the justice of created beings is lopsided. That of the Creator is infallible: it is the very equilibrium of the Universe in the physical, moral, or spiritual realms. If I do not see any motives for the hate I suffer or for the insults, this merely means I am near-sighted. I must in any case forgive, because a fire is not put out by adding fuel to it.

Solomon stated, and Paul the apostle to the Gentiles repeats: "If your enemy is hungry, give him food; if he is thirsty, give him drink. For in so doing you will heap burning coals upon his head." The hardened rabbis probably saw in this saying a refinement of immaterial vengeance. The Fathers of the Greek Church probably believed it meant that one must be irreproachable so that our enemies will attract to themselves all the reaction of their anger. The author of the Vulgate (St Jerome) understood it in a more Christian sense because he believed these coals are burning only from the fire of remorse and shame. Yes, the painful pardon to which I subject my wounded self-esteem is a light that will later cause remorse, repentance, and penance to germinate within the heart of my enemy.

After all, I am only offended because I am vulnerable. A tenacious desire for friendship, homage, respect, and possessiveness still persists within me. I would like others to believe me to be superior. If nothing mattered to me except obeying God, who could ever wound me? What demon, god, or man? And is there not but one sole, faithful, definite, and ever-increasing friendship—that of my Lord Christ?

Observance: In spite of everything, keep my feelings, my thoughts, and the expression on my face serene.

†

Feverish Haste

"Believe me, heaven and earth must disappear sooner than one iota, one flourish disappear from the law; it must all be accomplished."
(Matthew 5:18)

ANYTHING badly done has almost always to be done over again. Haste merely results in waste of strength and time. Men demand that I succeed. The Father asks only for my goodwill and for my efforts to be sincere. A work done perfectly and conscientiously satisfies the Law.

Whether I am an artist, a clerk, a thinker, or a workman, I will take the time to carry out my work thoroughly and, with all my skill, all my enthusiasm, all my clarity. If I spare myself the smallest stroke, the least research, pitiless destiny will oblige me to redo my work someday. In order to saturate my work with the maximum of beauty, energy, or truth, must I not build for it a perfect body and breathe a living soul into it? Are not long exhausting days and long nights fraught with anguish and supplications necessary?

The turbulent individual bestirs himself only to satisfy his mania for novelty, to escape boredom, or to satisfy an overwhelming covetousness. I must calm my volatility, if only to see more clearly. I will become calm, especially because outbursts of the self are always fomenters of discord, inwardly as well as outwardly. It is good at times to force ourselves to wait in the antechamber of the self. *Le temps ne respecte pas ce que l'on fait sans lui* (That which is done without due respect to time does not last). If the projects born with the most evident clarity come from God, He will not take exception if I defer their execution until such time as I feel they are ripe—for God has given me a critical or fine sense of evaluation. After all, is it right for me to believe myself pure enough, sufficiently upright, to receive providential solicitations without distorting them somewhat?

Observance: Never leave any work till I have completed it.

✝

The Temptations of Christ

> "He remained forty days and forty nights in the desert
> and was tempted by Satan; He lodged with the beasts,
> and the angels came and ministered to Him."
> (Mark 1:13)

MAN CAN COMMIT evil either from within himself or because he is spurred on to it by some external agent. This agent might be the natural seduction of some creature, or it might operate through an attack by one of the sides of darkness. This latter possibility, however, is quite rare. It occurs only in the case of very advanced disciples. Moreover, even among the saints, only very few have been approached by the perverse halo of the Great Rebel. Jesus is the only "Man" with Whom Satan talked in the open—unmasked. To attack Him, Satan surrounded himself with the infernal elite. This had to be so, because all creatures must at least once come face to face with the Word, so that they may perceive Truth—also, because no one is ever lost forever.

The man who is first to accomplish something entirely new expends a great deal of energy to achieve it. His imitators copy him, and follow his footsteps with less effort. That is the reason why, during the course of what is known of His life, as well as during the lightning-pierced darkness of His unknown life, Christ has performed every kind of act that human beings will ever be called upon to accomplish. That is why He endured all possible states of soul. That is why He has given thought to all sciences, all inventions, all masterpieces. Truly, He climbed all summits and crossed all mires. He has been everywhere.

A goodly portion of old elements are contained even in the least foreseen of circumstances, no matter what kind they are. Moreover, the adversary with whom I come in contact is always of a force equal to mine. And finally, no matter what the effort or struggle may be, Christ has for a certainty already executed the one and sustained the other, since that is what He came for.

Observance: In the midst of my fears, perplexities, and terrors, I will call with calm and confidence upon Him Who by anticipation underwent everything on my behalf already two thousand years ago.

Greed

> "With what difficulty will those who have riches
> enter the Kingdom of Heaven!"
> (Mark 10:23)

JESUS SAID: "It is easier for a camel to pass through the eye of a needle than for one who trusts in his riches to enter the Kingdom of God." Now, I can be avaricious and greedy without being wealthy. It is neither my work nor my state in life that will classify me in the spiritual hierarchy, but the intention with which I will have accomplished the one and fulfilled the other.

Any passion is greedy. The fanatic collector, the Don Juan, and the erudite adore various aspects of the same idol: possessiveness. Each one of us, whether it be due to our pre-existing merits or as a necessary test of the solidity of our virtues, receives from destiny a certain amount of bliss. This bliss might come in the form of natural gifts, fortune, friendships, or success. But as the saying goes, if we are offered an inch, we take a mile. And yet everything in Creation is measured. Whoever grabs happiness, money, or any other item whatever it be, deprives others of it. No matter whether the monopolist or the despoiled have ever met, in the moral realm all are present to all—and the groans of the cheated poison the happiness of the ostentatious extorters.

Gold is a curse to everything it contacts. Its fascination

blinds men to spiritual lights. The rich man should consider himself as the trustee of his wealth, even if he has acquired it through his own labor. Hence, I will take only what I need. But when I give I will imitate our maternal Nature, which always adds something superfluous to her gifts. In any case, to the shared gift I will add the superfluity of a smile and my affectionate greetings. I will also make use of the treasures of the unjust Mammon only with discretion.

Observance: Never amass unproductive treasures.

†

In Search of Praise

*"The men of this generation resemble children as
they sit in the marketplace, who call to one another:
We have played the flute and you have not danced;
we have sung mournful songs and you have not wept."*
(Luke 7:32)

To seek approbation is a mania, the candor of which readily brings me to smile when it applies to others—but I do not see it when in myself. Seekers of celebrity and renown set wheels cleverly in motion to obtain numerous votes, but be assured that they are held responsible for such vain maneuvers. Given that they are hunters after illusion, some day destiny will force them to feed upon illusions.

Are we Stoics? If so, what matters blame or praise when we only seek for the testimony of our own conscience? So, popularity and reputation appear as nothing but the tactical means needed to influence the crowds. When we have finally stopped believing in the primacy of will, let us then beware of praise, and even more so of flattery. If in our quest we surround ourselves with those who flatter, we open ourselves to the emanations of their heady appeal, from which we can only escape if we are either very strong, or very small.

The commendations we receive may be sincere or they

may be hypocritical. In the former there is a fresh perfume that makes them more dangerous to our modesty than the hypocritical ones. Were we wise, we would regard any compliment as a snare. Even the affection our friends feel towards us may be only partial. After all, is it not in the interest of the flatterers to seduce us for their own ends? If we wish to judge ourselves rightly, we must take the stand not to seek praise, and to abstain from blaming anyone. Other kinds of effort in the same vein may perhaps be attempted later, but for our present strength, maintaining a simple, reserved attitude quite suffices to give us a clearer mind and a more independent character.

Observance: Shun adulation and publicity.

✝

Desire for Show

"They perform all their deeds to win the esteem of men."
(Matthew 6:2)

WE DO NOT JUDGE apparel at its true value. Being a slave to style and fashion is either vanity or stupidity if we are impelled by conceit, perversity, or social-climbing. Even the dandy reaches but a superficial summit! And yet we must dress, decorate our home, and maintain a certain household in keeping with our social position. There again, conscience should be our guide.

We also need courage. Women know that a day will come when makeup will cease to hide their wrinkles. Men know that someday their tailor will be unable to hide their faulty posture or bulgy figures. Moreover, death is on the way, yet we continue to wear blindfolds, we hang on to everything we have craved for that is now escaping us, the loss of which we are not willing to accept.

I do not mean to imply that virtue should be ridiculous or peevish. Inner dignity always shines through our physical demeanor. When our thoughts are lofty, our clothing takes on a tailor's cut. The wise man leads an average life with a resplendent heart. While around some supermen the nimbus of summits floats sufficiently visible so as to endow the simple garb they wear with an astounding and moving nobility. But as for myself, whose mediocre soul cannot

Weekly Meditations

attain either the azure heights nor be sunk in the mud, who am merely "lukewarm," nourish so many desires, and accomplish so few deeds—I must shun affectation as well as coarseness and follow ordinary customs, conventions, and hygiene. I will not allow myself to be eccentric. This only fits exceptional souls; it is part and parcel of their character. It bears remembering in this connection that the tree in the forest which is taller than the others is also the one most exposed to storms and lightning.

Observation: Seek anonymity.

†

The Teachings of Christ

"It is the Father Who sent me, that commanded me what words I was to say, what message I was to utter."
(John 12:49)

When a man teaches, he may spread error. More to the point, he may not impart the opportune truth, the truth all his auditors are ready to receive, the truth suited to their present state, their future development, their environment, and their posterity. No one attains perfection. This is more true in the field of spiritual teaching than in any other.

Jesus, however, did possess perfect Truth, with all of its perfect applications, since the Word *is* this Truth. Knowledge is nothing but the mental image of Being. Because Jesus knows all those whom He addresses through and through—from their very center to their ultimate limitations, from their ante-secular origin to their post-secular end—He can tell each and all just what they need to know about this Absolute that He incarnates. My words float in and around me for a certain length of time, then dissolve and disappear. By contrast, the words of the Word, being Life, implant themselves into all hearts, and just like the seeds found in the Egyptian necropolis, are always ready to germinate.

Because Life is not an abstraction, in it everything is

active, real, spontaneous. Life is a kind of dynamite: the more resistance it meets, the more it intensifies, magnifies, and then explodes. Hence, for us who in our discourses possess nothing but a reflection of this intangible energy, it is through our acts that we will give our convictions the strongest existence. Good example is the best sermon and the finest of prayers.

Powers, science, and all other kinds of clarity can descend only in proportion to the degree the finite leaves room within myself for the infinite. This is the uniquely efficacious method that regenerates me—from my body up to the still virgin summit of my spirit. Through it alone I may become a temporary guide for those others who may have gone astray.

Observance: Each morning upon awakening I will read a verse from the Gospel as attentively as if I were opening the book for the first time.

†

Slander

> "What defiles a man is that which comes out of him, for it is from out of the heart of men that evil thoughts proceed…"
> (Mark 7:20–21)

MAN IS MADE in such a way that he can neither conceive nor perceive anything that comes from the outside unless he already possesses its counterpart within himself. The beauty of music moves me only because my sensitivity already comprises and contains its inner harmonies. And ugliness shocks me by a reverse mechanism. I cannot help seeing the vices or faults of my neighbors, but do I not carry the same morbid germs? What right have I to criticize, scorn, or publicize these faults? Slander is pusillanimous meanness, treachery. If I believe my neighbor is acting badly, why not tell him to his face when we are alone? Moreover, I am only responsible for those beings who have been entrusted to my care.

To speak of evil propagates evil. I will bear responsibility for the criticisms, sneers, and vexations a third party will hold against those who are absent because of my slanderous remarks. And for what reason? For a mere gesture, the intention or motive of which I know nothing? Am I truly able to evaluate the value of my own actions? Do I even discern the true nature of my deepest motives?

Weekly Meditations

To judge should mean to compare by means of an exact inner criterion. But since I am not perfect, my criterion is inevitably defective. Somewhere there is always a soul greater than I am. By saying "I certainly would never commit such an act!" I raise a challenge to evil, for evil is alive. It will hear the challenge and respond in kind—and be assured, blusterers are usually defeated. Thus, by bearing down upon others I enchain myself, force myself to a setback or to a standstill that will persist until such time as the play of circumstances permits me to make amends for my wrongdoing.

Observance: Never say anything evil about anyone who is absent.

✝

Falsehood

> "He abides not in truth since there is no truth in him;
> when he utters falsehood, he is only uttering
> what is natural to him."
> (John 8:44)

WHY DID THE Absolute, when He manifested as Creator and Savior, allow men to call Him the Word? Speech hides here a redoubtable mystery that—one may only guess—is saturated with life. The more true are my spoken words, the more fecund is that life. My words should be an exact image and a sincere expression of my inner motives. If I achieve this, my inner life will be alive and true—i.e., commensurate with its conformity to the Law, the Supreme Law, the Reason of the World, the creative Word. By contrast, ruse and hypocrisy serve nothing but evil—illicit processes can result only in an appearance of good. The chemist knows quite well how to extract a medicine from a poisonous juice, but what proof have I that these scientific therapeutics might not have cured one form of disease only to have it replaced with another?

Man is an incomprehensible mystery to man. God alone knows man because He created him. As mediocre as I am, I unite within myself all extremes. I bring together the antipodes. I carry within myself the worst microbes of spiritual

Weekly Meditations

Nothingness as well as the shining seed of perfect Being. I am the plaything of all breaths, while being at the same time the sole master of my own destiny. Hence a falsehood that creates a scission between an inner feeling and an outer expression is nothing else but a moral suicide. It poisons some of the lights and virtues within me. It also withers some lights and virtues in those to whom it is addressed.

If I respect my own words, never misusing them for anything useless, false, selfish, or wicked, my speech will be purified. Little by little it will recover its native energy. It will become creative and magical again. For those who ask help of me, it will be for them what the Word of God is to me: an active and vivifying blessing.

Observance: I will be sincere in thought, in words, and in actions.

†

Slander

"They stood there, loudly accusing Him."
(Luke 23:10)

To SLANDER, to accuse someone of a wrong he has not committed, is to commit murder, to assassinate. For what is bound in a particular place of the universe can only be unbound in the same place at a later date. The expiation of a slander demands that the aggressor, the victim, and the witnesses be reunited—whether here on Earth or elsewhere—in a set of analogous circumstances, and that the slanderer then asks and obtains pardon.

On the other hand, the victim of slander should not be irritated, distressed, or surprised by it. In actuality, no one can attack me unless I myself have given him the right—i.e., unless my destiny has authorized it. Strictly speaking, everything is just. Injustices are justices whose causal roots we do not see. Let us extract the almond from its bitter shell. One thing is certain: it is I who sowed these humiliations and ordeals in the past, and there is nothing for me to do now but reap them. Hence, I will not fall prey to tyrannical passions that despoil, and whose unsatisfied demands would reduce all men to slavery. Christ was right when He said: "God alone is good." We are fundamentally evil. In how many circumstances have I not been wicked? If I were to draw up the list of sufferings I have imposed upon those who were close to me, upon animals, plants, and even things; of all the times I have despised the beauty of life, insulted the charms of life; sown rancor and hate, or wrenched from innocence a more frightful scream than that of anger—yes, were I to draw up that list, how quickly would I move to hide my shame from my so-called defamers! I would repeat the followings words of an "unknown servant" of Heaven, to whom slanders about himself had been related: "Oh! They will never tell all the evil that there is to tell about me!"

Observance: I must defend those who are being slandered, rehabilitate them, and point out their virtues.

The Miracles of Jesus

*"No one could do the miracles you are doing,
unless God were with him."*
(John 3:2)

THERE ARE TWO kinds of miracles: natural miracles produced by unknown natural powers that bring into operation physical laws that are not yet discovered, and supernatural miracles that are due to direct divine intervention. The unknown powers of Creation may belong to the human being, to Nature, or to the Darkness. Divine intervention may be spontaneous, or it may come as an answer to prayer.

Among other matters, esotericism studies the means of producing natural miracles. But these practices, always partial, because they are human, often launch disorder into the immaterial atmospheres, and cause, in the normal development of beings and things, long-term disturbances far more pernicious than the evil the initiate wanted to cure. Magnetism, spiritualism, and magic are not infernal things, but they are things into which Hell can easily enter. Moreover, the will power indispensable to the adept for such operations facilitate the snares of the Adversary all the more.

Perfect man will be the king of Creation. We will have the legitimate right of command over Nature only when Nature sees that we have become masters of ourselves—i.e., when we have followed the school of the Gospel to the end. To possess a spiritual power from birth signifies that it is normal, but in addition that it entails the duty of exercising it for good only, never using it as a source for material gain. In just this way all of the powers of Jesus were innate, spontaneous. They radiated effortlessly, surpassing ancient magic and future wisdoms, just as the nearest infinite surpasses the greatest finite. And yet He never operated a miracle without first asking for the Father's permission.

Observance: Before performing any deed, ask the Father what His good pleasure is.

✝

Misanthropy

"There was a multitude seated all round Him."
(Mark 3:32)

WHEN THE SOCIETY of my fellowmen becomes unbearable, let me feel that I should not run away from them, but that here lies an opportunity for my patience to increase, that because of the effort it costs me perhaps my amiability will make unforeseen ameliorations possible in those whose presence riles me. The smallest things are important. The mere exchange of a glance with a passerby may exert a mysterious influence over him, upon me, and upon those who witness. To refuse going to gatherings expresses a kind of scorn. Remember that all plants yield fruits conformable to their species. Making an effort to be amiable when I have sorrows, or when I am in a morose mood, will distract me or counteract this lack. It will strengthen me, whereas solitude would only increase my sorrow and make my character still more vulnerable. In any case, why shouldn't people merit my attention? I only see the mask they wear. Their real being escapes me. The cleverest of soothsayers never really catch more than a glimpse of some of the apparent characteristics of their consulters. There is not a man or creature who is useless. From one and all I can take a lesson.

And after all, my tastes change faster than the shape of

the wind-driven clouds. The very ones who irk me today might be the ones for whom tomorrow I will forsake my duties so as to "run after them." Is it not plain wisdom to follow the school of life in the order of its successive lessons, and to do each thing in its proper time?

Finally, my Master, He in Whose intelligence all ideas were contained, Whose heart reflected and radiated all nobility, Whose gaze saw through all miseries—He for Whom the society of humans was certainly a perpetual martyrdom—has He not endured the cowards, the fools, the slothful, and the vainglorious?

Observance: I must abstain from judging anyone from the outward appearance of their personality.

Disgust with Life

"I have prayed for thee, that thy Faith may not fail."
(Luke 22:32)

SADNESS CAN BECOME so deeply ingrained that it may even take away the false courage of committing suicide. Yet, if I have understood anything about the meaning of life, I know it is not success that elevates me, but all the efforts I earlier made. I know it is not the love I have received that embellishes my soul, but the love I have given. I know it is not science per se that develops intelligence, but the work expended in acquiring that science.

I despair only because we are too concerned about our self. Where does one find the man capable of giving up his hopes and preferences continuously? Educators can do nothing more than suggest to our will higher and still higher incentives, in proportion as we advance, indefinitely. The Imitation of Christ, "the most wonderful book that ever came from the hands of men," is anything else but an inner gymnastics enabling us to escape the grasp of earthly sorrows.

The Gospel alone dares show me what is the supreme goal. It alone dares tell me that I will reach this goal precisely by means of the energy I spend pursuing the provisional, successive goals that are the culminating crests of the world, the summits of my own nature—and as such, subject to change and death. If I vitalize that expended energy with my intention of reaching God, I transmute it. I transpose it from the temporal to the eternal. In any situation and on any kind of mental plane this intention remains forever accessible to me, because God remains, in short, my principle and my goal. When ordinary ambitions and joys will have lost their savor, so much the better. Once these mirages are dissipated, my method will become that much more lucid and serene. No more will idols be able to stop me. The disciple knows his Master is always close by. That is why for him suffering becomes the blessed breath that fans the spiritual flame of his love.

Observance: Have faith in the future.

†

Despair

> "My soul is sad unto death... Yet Father,
> not what I will but what Thou wilt."
> (Mark 14:34–36)

THE FATHER FORBIDS destiny from burdening anyone beyond his strength. What makes my chains seem heavy comes from my believing that they are unjust—as also comes from my secret hope that I can rid myself of them. But the contortions I execute to this end serve only to wound me, and as I thus wear myself out, they seem still more unbearable.

It takes so little to lose courage. Courage is not an abstract entity, but an organ of my psychic personality. It possesses a form. It has an existence of its own, as real as my hands and feet. Just as a muscle is strengthened and develops through exercise, so all intellectual and moral faculties—among which is courage—are developed when they are engaged and wither when left inactive. If I am in despair, if I do not find the ingenious method or the decisive energy that would help me today, it is because I have not known how to will in the past. The strong south winds compel the tree to strengthen its fibers; hardships compel man to expend his energies.

I must not desire death anymore than I should desperately cling to life. I have no right to do either. My body does not belong to me; it is not I who has erected it. Dare I consider myself wiser than the governing laws of the Universe?

The dark angel of despair whispers to me that I have been abandoned. Yes, it is true that friends sometimes leave me—those whom I love and those who love me. But not for an instant does the One Who has undertaken to lead me to the goal ever lose interest in my fate. His angels are always by my side. Without their being aware of it, even those poor men who refuse this constant offer of help are protected and watched over by the Shepherd from afar.

Observance: I must try to forget my worries for a few minutes each day.

✝

The Transfiguration

"Lord, how good for us to be here!"
(Matthew 17:4)

ONE DOES NOT give wine to little children. So when Heaven dissimulates itself beneath the undecipherable entanglements of cause and effects, or behind the veils of the physical, intelligible, as well as invisible worlds, it is because its splendor, if laid bare, would prove too dazzling for my weakness. No one can see God without dying. Were my eyes limpid, were my gaze able to pierce the millennia-old walls of the spiritual prison where I have incarcerated myself, I would recognize that my sufferings cannot repair the harm I have caused. I would find out that evil is extraordinarily prolific in this wicked world whose purified humus suits it to a "t." For in truth I am constantly despoiling some creature or other, and if I had to pay my debt down to its last bitter penny, along with its compounded interest, I would never see the end of my labor. But the Father's Mercy indemnifies His justice.

Were I to go forward towards Supreme Goodness solely by my own efforts, the road would be endless. But with each paltry step I take towards Him, my Savior rushes to meet me, swift as the lightning I take to be a sign of His wrath, whereas it is only the anger of some demon from whom Love has just snatched a prey.

Weekly Meditations

Mystical raptures, delights, and ecstasies are nothing more than faraway smiles of this Love that only my lukewarmness keeps from reaching me. Doubtless, Love shines under diverse forms through the magnificence of the world. But these forms are merely there to offer an encouraging prod to make up for my lackadaisical slackness.

The Friend is always to be found, and is closest to me in my grief, during times of poverty, behind unhappiness, crime, acridities, and inner solitudes. He is at the bottom of everything troubling my heavy soul, for He came for the sick and He will never come except for them.

Observance: Before making any decision, I will lay human wisdom aside and ask myself: What would Jesus do in my place?

†

Heedlessness

"Who is it you are looking for?"
"Jesus of Nazareth."
"It is I."
(John 18:4–5)

CARELESSNESS, DISTRACTION, forgetfulness, inaccuracy, imprudence, improvidence, inconstancy, thoughtlessness—all are failings stemming from lack of attention. They lead to discouragement, exhaustion, and failure. To increase our power of attention means that we must draw from unlimited patience, begin without fanfare, without shock, but gently, with tenacity. The least detail is important. The least obstacle must receive my minutest care. Acts, emotions, thoughts, and words project into the secondary atmosphere a dynamic emanation that after a long and winding way returns to its point of departure. Any concentration produces in the volatile organism a void-point or vacuum to which these little comets are drawn. Thus are born those bothersome associations of ideas that come when we want to abstract ourselves in work.

Adepts possess methods that increase the power of attention, calm turmoil, and liberate thought. Recent trends of mentalism, psychism, and personal magnetism have appropriated all they could from Eastern psychology. But all of this is nothing but artifice and a transplantation that abuses energies. Man has no right to lift a force from its proper domain to install it elsewhere. In attempting such a thing he no doubt believes himself very clever, but in fact he is nothing but a destroyer, a tyrant, one who sows disorder. We human beings are like all other creatures: it is from the center that we develop, not from the circumference—and that center is the heart. Whatever it may have been in former times, the training of the attention is no longer a lopping off, but the normal cultivation of the rich soil of material tasks under the vivifying rays of the sun of goodwill. It does not kill anything; it consolidates, organizes, and unifies.

Observance: I must never allow myself to give in to daydreaming or to inaction.

✝

Obstinacy

*"Jesus reproached the eleven for their unbelief
and their obstinacy of heart."
(Mark 16:14)*

OBSTINACY IS NOT the same as will. To will means to do all that which judicious reasoning indicates as opportune with our body, intelligence, and even our passions. A person of goodwill sees clearly. A stubborn person sees one point only. He does not admit that another might think rightly. Rather, in his view everyone should think as he does. And in this regard, am I myself not often enough convinced that I hold the only truth, at least on a few subjects? Even when an opinion is exact, it is far better to blunt its cutting edges rather than start endless discussions that might offend, and in any case probably not persuade, our opponent. All truths need not be told. If I obstinately set out to satisfy a purely personal desire against one and all, I risk embarrassment and pitfalls, for this obstacle that so irritates me and makes me impatient is actually a warning. Or rather, this particular irascible impatience I experience should point out that my project is not right.

If I confine myself to following obsolete methods, I am "pawing the ground"—merely marking time. One must of course respect the opinion of elderly people, but if to an old man the period of his youth appears to have been almost

Weekly Meditations

irreproachable, still it had its own wrongdoings. The difference between yesterday and today is slight, though it is in any case always to the advantage of the present, since evolution always marches on. The only trouble is that I see just the edge of things, just the nooks and crannies from out of this multitude of one's own personal progress. Hence, I judge badly.

If I refuse to pay a visit, if I refuse an idea or a book, those are two doors I am closing: one to myself and one to the thing offered me. Therefore, I will welcome and examine everything presented to me with clear judgment, comparing it all to the model Jesus offers me. Nothing will be able to seduce me except Jesus, Who personifies the Ideal of all.

Observance: Mistrust my own opinions.

Anxiety

"The morrow will take care of itself."
(Matthew 6:34)

FEAR, EVEN IN its most attenuated forms, weakens our moral and physical bodies. What have I to fear, since nothing happens without God's permission? Nothing happens unless I have deserved it. Nothing happens unless it is for my good. No one truly and spiritually stronger than I can attack me. If I could only see how many things and forces have collaborated in order that I might be born, that I might eat a meal, that I might cross this thoroughfare, I would then understand how precious my life is and how profoundly my Friend loves me.

But I would have no other merit thereby than that of being reasonable. My Friend does not crave a reasonable friendship, a natural friendship. He wants me to enter into the supernatural with Him—there, where reason does not hold sway, where there is neither logic nor customs. He wants me to enter into His love. That is why He leaves me in ignorance.

These worries that so debilitate me are reasonable—which is just why I should suppress them. If I am attacked by a highwayman, it means that I also have been a brigand. If my associate cheats me, it is due to my having betrayed trusts. Man reaps what he has sown. Anxiety spreads havoc in one's intelligence, blinds intuition, attracts the very misfortune, illness, or failure that it fears.

If duty calls me, even the clear presentiment of a catastrophe must not deter me from following my path, since I am in the hands of God. I will be neither pusillanimous, nor rash. Calmness attracts luck and spreads it; it thwarts intrigues, dissipates obstacles. Calmness is the herald of inner life. What can possibly trouble me, since the Master walks with me?

> *Observance*: Ask the Word for help, and then walk straight on to meet the obstacle.

✝

The Last Supper

"Such is the bread which has come down from Heaven."
(John 6:58)

THE WORD FEEDS the Universe. All creatures owe their existence to Him. They subsist only because He gives Himself to them perpetually through a sacrifice renewed *ad infinitum*.

This is the way a pantheist understands the relationship between God and the world, and how he explains the rite of the Eucharist. The Christian, however, believes the Last Supper to have a higher meaning, a more precise and living virtue. He is right in believing this. He is even more infinitely right than he imagines. Take the first hypnotist who comes along, an average man as far as his inner life is concerned. It is possible for him to make his subject experience all sorts of sensations from a glass of pure water. Could not Christ, the first among all beings, could He not confer upon bread and wine the very virtues, the totality of which constitute His own personality? This explanation, however, is only an outer exegesis. When He said, "This is my Body, this is my Blood," Jesus transmuted and recreated the spiritual essence of the vine and of the wheat. And there is still something more. In His hands, matter is not inert dust. Thus I foresee that gradually and in proportion to my greater inner attainments, the truer and more genuine facets of the mystery of transubstantiation will be revealed to me.

Moreover, when for our sake the Word made Himself flesh and created an individuality with which He clothed Himself and began His descent, He did so at the price of unspeakable suffering. During His descent, the deeper He penetrated into matter, the more did universal crime martyr Him. The Word, so to speak, authorized Himself to choose only those elements from the sufferings of His divine nature in order to form His human nature. "His body is food" because it has been formed through the laboring pains of His divine descent. "His blood is drink" because His agonies have vitalized His works.

Observance: Once a day, I must impose upon myself some self-sacrifice for a charitable cause, in remembrance of Christ.

Prayer

"While He stood praying, the Heaven was opened…"
(Luke 3:21)

JESUS TELLS ME that long speeches are not necessary when speaking to God. As I can and should refer all my material and spiritual needs to Him, I must also ask Him for His help even when it seems possible to me to rely solely upon my own forces. Few words are necessary in any case, because He is well aware of my needs long before I set them forth. However, just because He so loves me, He likes for me to lean upon Him.

He is infinitely above any kind of eloquence. Therefore I will speak to Him in simple terms. He is present in all the emotions I may feel as I invoke Him and in all the favors that may ensue. To make this possible He proportions His splendor to my lowliness and shrinks His greatness to my littleness. That is why He is closer when inner delights do not come, as well as when the extreme center of my heart is fixed solely upon Him. For then He comes to me with a degree of light just surpassing that which my unworthy nature can perceive and bear. Whenever I feel I am in an arid, languorous, and solitary state, if I continue to cling with an indefectible grasp to Christ, this night of my nature will become the dazzling day of faith. This is the time when I am given the chance to surpass myself, whereas the fervors and ecstasies I experience are but the pleasures of my personality enjoying its state.

No matter how high I may rise, God is higher still. Whenever I feel His touch, it is because He stoops down to encourage me. Thus it is that my prayer will be heard only if I am humble. Hence I must abase myself ever lower in order to meet Him Who, being the All Highest, has come down to Nothingness just for me. Humility is the cornerstone of one's whole inner edifice. It is the atmosphere of the disciple.

Observance: Daily, I will meditate upon one of the petitions of the Lord's Prayer.

☦

Charity

"You should love one another, as I have loved you."
(John 15:12)

ALL SPIRITUAL VIRTUES are really but one virtue. Whoever possesses one has all the others. But charity is the foremost virtue God asks of me because among them all it is the one I can make the most precise efforts to acquire. Charity takes innumerable forms. If that fire is burning in my heart, all my actions, words, and thoughts will become offerings and alms. If that fire does not burn therein, I still have the inestimable resource of acting, speaking, and thinking as if I loved. This is the divine falsehood to which I must constrain myself at all times and in all situations.

Charity is neither benevolence nor philanthropy. These are human, prudent, and reasonable, whereas charity is rash. It consults nothing but its own compassion. No obstacle stands in its way. No ingratitude rebuffs it. No reward excites it. Intuitively, it knows all niceties, speaks all tongues. It places itself on the level of any and all conditions. Thanks to it, I will be able to reach even the confines of the Universe. Through it, God obligates Himself to serve me. Out of charity, God has created the world, and recreates it. It is charity that forms the body of the Son of Man and the soul of the Son of God. Through charity all miracles become possible, all mysteries are unveiled, all the chains of matter are shattered.

Now, this principle of all powers, this source of all beauties, this secret of all deliverance, is among all the virtues the only one for which I will use the same discipline and rigor as one who is training to be an athlete. In the cultivation of the other virtues, something escapes my control, whereas a gesture, a thought, a word of help for a creature in distress are always subject to my conscience, and possible to my will power.

Observance: Never let a day go by without helping someone in one way or another.

Humility

> "He is greatest in the Kingdom of Heaven who
> will abase himself like this little child."
> (Matthew 18:4)

IN ITS ESSENCE, humility does not consist in the knowledge I may have of my weakness or wickedness, in my being conscious of divine grandeurs, in a search for menial tasks or an obscure existence performing exhausting toils, in accepting scorn, in public avowal of my sins, in forgetfulness of the good I might have done, in the pleasure one experiences in seeing others succeed or being preferred, or in the certitude of being the least among men. All these things are but acts of humility, the conditions or fruits of humility. Besides being all this, however, humility is something else I can sense but not quite define. When one believes one is humble, one ceases to be so. Humility is a mystery in the center of my being, a limitless and fathomless mystery. All the virtues are based upon and live from humility. It is through humility and because of humility that it becomes possible for God to dwell in me. It is up to God to establish humility within me insofar as my incurable pride permits Him to do so.

To prepare myself to receive this gift, I will try to understand that it is God Who accomplishes in me and through me all the good I do—and that the evil I do comes from me. I will thank Him for everything: happiness and unhappiness, gifts and disabilities. I will let others see His benefactions only as a help to them. Praises will sadden me. I will rejoice when criticized. I will hide the failures of others. I will not seek for positions in the public eye. I will not be vain. I will not fear ridicule. I will ask my Master to reveal me to myself, to let me see that particular secret perversity of which I am not always aware—but know to be in me—and which poisons all the good I want to do.

Observance: I must cultivate the feeling of humility within myself rather than express it through artificial gestures.

✝

Death and Resurrection of Jesus

"Father, into Thy hands I commend my spirit."
(Luke 23:46)

MY ACTUAL STATE of being is both my workshop and my battlefield. The stirrings of my passions tend to translate themselves into acts. They feel that they must incarnate in order to subsist, and that if I do not take care to build for them a very concrete body they become extinct. The material existence I give to these immaterial essences subsequently reacts from within upon the world itself, upon this imponderable that saw them born. But the primary, as well as the general, law is that nothing happens in the visible realm which does not already exist in the invisible. The visible phenomena, the proceedings, meetings, and harangues that occur, whether for an illness or for an enterprise or in a revolution, are but puppets put in motion by a hidden hand.

Since Christ wanted to give the world a living example, He complied submissively to the law of the world, a law He had promulgated in the past: He worked with His hands, underwent suffering in His body, visited everywhere, even the kingdom of the dead. Death is a living goddess, and she is the strongest of all. She triumphed over her immortal sisters until that singular night when for the first time she met defeat. She, too, had to obey her Lord. The long expectation of the ancient Justice had to come to an end so that they might ascend to Heaven. It was necessary to make possible the future resurrection of the flesh, that mysterious transmutation of our coarse, crippled organisms into impassible, radiant bodies.

No matter how dark may be the shadows where creation slumbers, there are dawns that bring it occasional light. Creation marches forward in spite of divisions, struggles, alternate excesses. It marches towards harmony and peace. There is only one Master: the One Who has traced all plans, grouped all masses, scoured all roads; the One Whom everything must obey, yet Who, because of His love for me, demands from me only the obedience of love (to show it to me, He even came down to me), and Who, finally returning to the Heights, invited me to follow Him.

Observance: Each morning, I will believe that, during the night, some evil has died in me, and that I am reborn purer for another effort.

†

Illness

> "He took our infirmities upon Himself,
> and bore our sicknesses."
> (Matthew 8:17)

Among all the systems proposed to establish a philosophy of medicine, only the religions tell the truth. An accident, vital disturbances, or pernicious heredity, are nothing but the "how" of it. The "because" is the domain of the merciful and just permissions the Father lets immanent Justice administer to let us feel the counter-blows of the licenses we have taken in the past. Sin is what makes my body vulnerable. An infraction of the Law is a malevolent force that circulates, sowing disorder through the invisible multitude of secondary causes, then to return fatally to its point of departure reinforced by everything (analogous to its venom) that has been able to adhere to it during its course. It is I who am the true author of my physiological blemishes and accidents.

It follows that only he can heal to whom Truth gives cognizance of the causes, and the power to remit sin. Any other medicine, no matter how mysterious or scientific it may be, only enchains the disease for either a short or long period. But this imprisoned disease always succeeds in breaking the chains and returning to its victim until the debt is at least approximately paid.

Weekly Meditations

And yet I have a duty towards my body—which is to bring it relief. After all, my body has been but the instrument. It is, rather, I, the self, my heart, my will and selfishness, that bear the greater responsibility. I will try to be cured, but will not make use of any means that would only be another fault, a new debt, and the principle of a future illness. Moreover, to all remedies I will add my prayers. And when I have recovered my health I will visit the sick, help them, pray for them, extend the hand of love and the compassion they merit—since my Master says that these people are: Himself.

Observance: I will try not to complain when suffering.

†

Mourning

"Leave the dead to bury the dead."
(Luke 9:60)

OUR BELOVED ONES whom death wrenches from us are not lost. Regardless of the frightful complexity of the world, everything finds its own place that much quicker when creatures let themselves be guided, whereas by *not* obeying, they delay this "putting in order" that religions call: the Judgment. If men could only see what happy consequences resignation engenders, if only they could see what disturbances occur in the dual motion of souls because of spiritualistic séances and obstinate regrets, they would peacefully await the hour to go and meet their departed ones. They would be satisfied with the spontaneous manifestations of survival that alone are licit and opportune. The immortal spirit does not need rest as often as the body does. When it has returned its instrument of labor to the Earth, it receives another in another world. All religions teach this. When this ultra-terrestrial life is expiatory, it is called either purgatory or hell. When it is a life of repose, it is called paradise.

When I weep for my departed ones, is it not merely the loss of the joy that their beloved presence gave me that I regret? But does not each one have his work? Does not the one who tries to prevent me from getting an education do me harm? The departed are attending a new school. I do not have the right to distract them or to pull them back. If I love them truly, I will leave them entirely free to perform their unknown tasks.

I weep for them because I love them; and I love them for the happiness, peace, and strength they gave me. It is thus that, through lures proportionate to my selfishness, industrious Nature gives me an interest in pure Love. Little by little Nature teaches me to love higher beings. It leads me kindly to the summit from where one discovers the horizons of sacrifice. Hence, I will remain united with my departed; no longer by external bonds, however, but by that very thing we both possess, something more central and permanent: love and the practice of doing Good.

Observance: Let me hide my sorrows when in mourning.

✝

The Fear of Death

"He who listens to my words, enjoys eternal life."
(John 5:24)

THE REASON WE fear death is not so much our apprehension of the unknown as because of the rupture of the myriad ties that bind our body, our sensitivity, and our character to this world. It seems as though we are losing everything we love, forever. And yet, there exist innumerable realms where landscapes are more beautiful, beings better, works more august, friendships more faithful. Nevertheless, our lack of confidence dominates the fear of the morrow. We refuse to accept that never would the kindness of the Father throw defenseless beings into isolation or into unmerited down-crushing.

The enemy has to be confronted. If I dare look death in the face, it will loose its horror. All that surrounds me, that is familiar and that I love, such as beings and objects, are only trusts I must administer or aids to my progress or students to whom I have a mandate to teach something. None of them belong to me. Nothing belongs to anyone, only to God. It is by God, through God, because of God, and for God that I am licensed to care for, perfect, and love those with whom I come in contact—whether people or things.

Even the beings I cherish most profoundly I cannot take along with me. Have I chosen them freely? No, I was drawn to them by something, something much stronger than my reason. Hence, no matter how deep my love of others may be, it is nothing but the sign of the true bond that unites them to me—a prior, solid bond that was tied by the strong hands of Angels upon the order of the Father.

We have known our beloved ones in former times. We will find them again later, even as we found them today. The more I advance, the quicker will fall the veils that hide the true faces of beings from me, and the more intimately will I be united, in the splendor of essential Reality, with those I love.

Observance: Think of death as the ever blessed liberator.

☦

The Ascension

*"Even as He blessed them, He parted from them,
and was carried into Heaven."*
(Luke 24:51)

A COMET EMERGES from the unexplorable depths of space; it descends to the nether abysses, encircles a star, then returns to the spheres above, all the while sowing new powers, regulating and reorganizing everywhere. In the same way, when the Word descends to the very depths of Nature, He promulgates precepts and gives examples, then returns to His abode by the new path He Himself has just hewn, and where all those whom He has called to follow Him during His course will one day travel. The Ascension completes the messianic work.

Never could man, even had he undergone all tribulations, have obtained passage from those who guard the darkest hells or those who guard the luminous paradises. The rebels who covet his body and spirit would always have invented some new ambush or insurmountable barrier. Christ, however, has opened a secret path. He has built bridges across chasms and placed lifeguards at the dangerous crossings.

Never for a moment does man walk without a guide. In all his acts invisible collaborators aid him. The tears he sheds are brought and laid as precious gems at the feet of the Lord. His prayers are always conveyed, from one sphere to another sphere, up to the eternal throne.

Thus the Ascension, which is nothing but a legend to the academic commentators, and nothing but the symbol of the final phases of the subjective attainment of the adept to the esotericists, appears rather to the one who knows Jesus as the ultimate sign of His solicitude, as the supreme effort of His Mercy. May the whole of humanity set forth upon this blessed road in one definite leap, and in one triumphal flight reach, as soon as ever can be, this unique summit that soars above everything, beyond everything, and yet is everywhere at the same time.

Observance: When I have a free moment, I will repeat to myself that Jesus asks me to follow Him.

†

Contempt

"You must not give that which is holy to dogs."
(Matthew 7:6)

EVEN IF I DID POSSESS all talents and knew all sciences, if I hold inferior beings, the pariahs, and unintelligent people in contempt, I prove myself stupid and hard-hearted thereby. In fact, what do my renown and success depend upon? Might it be from an ounce of phosphorous or iron in my organism, from a gesture of my guardian angel, from a word or a meeting, from the secret devotion of some friend, visible or invisible? I wonder! How do I know?

If I live outside the pale of society or at the bottom rung of the social ladder, I have no right to despise their underpinnings. There is always a just reason for everything. If things seem disorderly, it merely appears so owing to the fact that my opera glasses are not in focus. All of us—rich, poor, good, wicked, ruffians, or intelligent people—we are taking classes. If we tease one another we lose the value of the teaching. Be assured, we will have to make up for the hours we have dissipated and pay for our disobedience.

If I believe myself to be innocent and just, I become sensitive to the least prick against my self-esteem. But if I recognize my worthlessness and see how little of this complex, inconsistent, and anemic personality belongs to me, the attacks will not affect me anymore. Rather, they will be like a thorn in a finger or a tear in my clothing: I will not become irritated, but joyfully continue my fortifying walk through the vast forest of the world with good humor. The humble do even better: they thank the Father; they know that each suffering is a little bit of impurity being washed away, a little bit of darkness being chased away by the sun. Does such heroism alarm my timorous courage? Well, at least I will abstain from believing myself superior and welcome the attacks with a smile of love and surrender.

Observance: Be kind towards everyone, even those whom I believe to be unworthy.

Criticism

> "Do not judge others,
> that you may not be judged."
> (Matthew 7:1)

No critic ever wins a sympathetic ear. Even were his remarks judicious, few will put them into practice. However, the man who is modest knows how to profit even from such partiality. In truth, an envious glance or a disdainful glance will always be of benefit to me because he who has ugliness in his character is an expert in ugliness. Indulgence does not see evil.

If circumstances place me in such a position that I in turn must judge some of my brothers, or some of their works, I know that Love will offer other methods. I know for example that Love does not tear down but builds something on the side, it constructs something else. I know that neither spoken nor written words possess the compelling force of example. I know that true humility (the secret conviction I have of my ignorance and lack of skill), though it may prevent me from seeing the defects in the works of others, will allow me to discover therein the outline of some new beauty and the seed of a force still unaware of itself. These new findings, being positive, are of far more importance than the hammerings of the wrecking-ball critic who only piles rubble upon rubble and further cracks an already tottering wall.

Weekly Meditations

I must permit myself no intolerance. I must respect the free will of another even if I am strong enough to constrain him. Why should my opinion be the best one, given that the number of possibilities and probabilities is infinite? If a desire to criticize wells up in me, I will put myself in the place of my brother, I will picture to myself his state of soul, his motives, his temperament, and his milieu. That will be an instructive study, as well as a step towards my own self-mastery. Thus will I learn to discover evil within the good I attribute to myself, and the good lying dormant in the evil I perceive in others.

Observance: Be tolerant; look for the good; point it out.

†

Impatience

"It is by patience that you will secure possession, of your souls."
(Luke 21:19)

ALL THE EVENTS from which destiny weaves the pattern of my existence are but exercises to develop my faculties. When a goal interests me, if I believe that by attaining it I will experience a profound joy, I feel capable of superhuman efforts. This kind of energy, however, is nothing but selfishness—I should be able to expand it towards goals that are of no profit to me. The perfect achiever acts (just as does the ambitious man) with all his might—but all the while remaining as impassible before defeat as before success.

Impatience is a loss of strength. Whether born from an external obstacle or from my own awkwardness, impatience does nothing but delay the objective I am pursuing, because it disturbs the lucidity of my reason and sometimes even that of my senses. And its ferment, which carries over into the future, makes the disillusionment that will follow my selfish success all the more bitter.

I am loaded down with the chains of time, space, and matter. I can only do what they permit me. Quite often they are salutary to me in the end because the mirage of the greedy happiness towards which I rush headlong often transforms itself into suffering the moment I reach it—just as a child who never believes his mother's counsel has first to experience a burn before he will stay away from the fire.

"What is done without due respect to time does not last." Patience, whether as constancy, endurance, resignation, waiting, indulgence, or gentility is the most efficacious of virtues, for it forces me to become master of myself. Patience imposes the attitude of immutability upon the febrile self. It gives my faculties the time to grow, especially those faculties whose existence I do not even suspect. It permits my learning the lessons of life in depth. In short, the primordial discipline for my will is no other than patience.

Observance: I must compel myself to be gentle with everyone.

†

Apparitions of Christ After His Death

"I am with you until the consummation of the world."
(Matthew 28:20)

THE REAL "how, whys, and wherefores" for the visits the Master paid to His disciples after His Resurrection escape my understanding. I only know that the witnesses were not hallucinating, that there is no question of legends or phenomena such as those produced by mediums, magnetisms, or magicians, because in Jesus the power is supernatural, whereas these latter seekers, no matter how intrepid they are or how strongly animated they may be by an admirable thirst for knowledge, can only grasp natural forces.

The reality of the Resurrection can be historically proven. But to me that should be inconsequential—otherwise, the Christ I imagine is not the true Christ. What are analyses good for, since I know He can do everything? His spirit is perpetually hovering. He is there at births, at deaths, at reconciliations. It is from Him that the unknown passerby I met received the startling radiance that moved me tenderly to my very depths. It is He Who gives to the glance, which I caught by chance, the miraculous virtue of leading my soul to the shores of eternal Beauty. It is because of Him that the frozen mantle of despair and worries falls from my shoulders on account of the smile of a child or of an old man I saw. If my yearning for Jesus animates my whole being, I will see the image of Jesus everywhere.

I know that Christ can manifest before me under any kind of form, that He may appear to me in dreams or in an ecstasy. I know that He can make Himself visible in flesh and blood simultaneously, in many places, and upon many worlds. He is the Master. He commands all substances and forms. He is everywhere. He is at my side with His whole Heaven. May I, dear God, at least never close my eyes or my heart to this marvelous encounter.

Observance: I will conduct myself in such a way that everything can tell me some word of Jesus.

†

Melancholy

"When you fast, do not show it by gloomy looks."
(Matthew 6:16)

MELANCHOLIA is a lack of desire brought on by fatigue, disappointments, or weakness. Most often it is the result of strenuous research or of having made foolhardy experiments. It might also come from fatigue owing to a tedious routine of life, shattered dreams, ugliness in our surroundings, or some renunciation not based upon Love. The "zest" that often facilitates my performing the daily chores is the "alcohol" poured out for me by some compassionate genii in order that I might at least for a time surmount my anxieties, because I am still not courageous enough to work by reason of sheer duty. I still need, alas! the fallacious attraction of desires that transfigure the ashes and give body to daydreams.

Eyes just opening to light remain tender for a long time. I must neither mock the forlorn dreamer nor the lazy, indolent man. All creatures serve in one way or another. Even if in spite of themselves, they do work. There are also other kinds of tasks than those I am able to perceive. Hence, I will not judge the unproductive, but instead attempt to be twice as productive myself.

Merriment denotes an over-brimming strength; it is the sign of physical and moral health. I must take hold of myself so that no one will see my sadness. I must not expect consolation from anyone except from the Consoler. If I treat it merely with joviality and outer distractions, my sadness will only be replaced by another kind of sadness. One can only be liberated from a debt by paying it, not by denying it.

To be perturbed by failure is unwise. If for instance I have worked for selfish ends, failure then becomes a grace since it shows up my vanity. If I have worked for an ideal, have I really done all I could? And after all, does not God know far better than I what is good for me?

> *Observance*: I must give of myself, of my life, if I wish to receive life.

†

Insubordination

*"Take my yoke upon yourselves…;
for my yoke is easy and my burden is light."*
(Matthew 11:29–30)

RESISTANCE, REFUSALS, debates, sulkiness, impatience, mutiny, grumbling, rebuffs, rebellion, and revolt—all are diverse phases of the spirit of personal egotism. The human being, even the god and the earthworm, are born here-below precisely for the purpose of learning to obey. God is the father of a family who asks of His children docility—not for His sake, but for theirs. He knows that revolt leads them to perdition. When He is certain of their submission, He gives them back their freedom—even more, He makes Himself their servant.

By considering all things profoundly, it is from God that everything flows. Neither the king, the minister, the policeman, the foreman, nor anyone else would have any authority over me unless God more or less immediately gave him the power. There again, it is I, the former "I," who gives to the present "I" the authorities to whom I must submit.

If my pranks of the past were such that I find myself today riveted to the yoke of oppressive regulations, whose fault is that? If the law tyrannizing me seems unjust, my revolt will only serve to tighten the bonds—and so my temporary victory over it will only engender a still more inexorable tyranny. Violence is not annihilated by the opposite violence: it merely changes form. The execution of a murderer does not purify his heart. Something else is necessary to do that.

If I am sufficiently master of myself to obey any order effortlessly, no one will ever have the power to control me. Life demands obedience from me only because revolt still dwells in me. Moreover, had I reached the state of perfect obedience—such as that of Angels—I still might have to obey seemingly spurious demands in order to offer the disobedient ones a living and pure example. Innocence alone is truly creative.

Observance: If I want to advance faster, I will try to obey not only my superiors, but my equals and my inferiors as well.

Perfection

*"You are to be perfect,
as your heavenly Father is perfect."*
(Matthew 5:48)

PERFECTION IS NOT to be found in impassability, in holding the works of Nature in contempt, in living a peculiar mode of life, in minute observances of piety, in long drawn out prayers, in physical chastisements, in scruples, in blind adherence to my own spirited views, in ecstasies, or in the gift of miracles. Perfection lies in conforming my will to the will of God, and in the energy deployed to subject my body, my brain, and my heart to this obedience. Perfection is as accessible to me as to everyone. God chooses as prophets, seers, and thaumaturges individuals whose physical and psychic organisms offer certain particular virtues and special properties for that purpose. But everyone has a heart he can purify and a self he must renounce.

God offers Himself to me. I must give myself to Him. By my will—whose principle is love—I begin this gift, which I will perfect by my actions. My first effort will be to purify my heart. My second effort will be to purify my whole being according to the indications offered to me by life.

Perfection is the absolute. All I can do is to set my heart upon it—but set my heart upon it, I must. I must relentlessly surpass myself. Perfection is the fulfillment of the self. And as I am a human being, my supreme fulfillment is in God, and in God alone. Perfection does not mean to be immersed in the ocean of the indefinite. Neither is it the exaltation of individuality. It is the development of all my powers brought to their very limits—meaning that upon this natural perfection descends the supernatural Perfection which comes, not to destroy it, but to create it anew; not to enlarge it further, but to transmute it, to transplant it upon the splendid and pure land that is called eternal Life.

Perfection is called Jesus Christ. The road to perfection is Jesus Christ. The strength to follow that path is Jesus Christ, Who is singular unity, innumerable multiplicity, inconceivable dream, indestructible reality. That is the goal of the Universe, the goal of my existence.

Observance: Each time I hear the clock strike the hour, I will ask God to light His Love within me.